SMYTHE GAMBRELL
LIBRARY

WESTMINSTER SCHOOL

PRESENTED BY

Jim Jerden

A FIRST LOOK AT ANIMALS WITHOUT BACKBONES

By Millicent E. Selsam and Joyce Hunt

ILLUSTRATED BY HARRIETT SPRINGER

WALKER AND COMPANY ✸ NEW YORK

For our special friend Claire

First published in the United States of America
in 1976 by the Walker Publishing Company, Inc.

Published simultaneously in Canada by Fitzhenry &
Whiteside, Limited, Toronto.

Trade ISBN: 0-8027-6268-9
Reinf. ISBN: 0-8027-6269-7
Library of Congress Catalog Card Number: 76-12056

Printed in the United States of America.

10   9   8   7   6   5   4   3   2   1

A *FIRST LOOK AT* SERIES

Each of the nature books for this
series is planned to develop the
child's powers of observation and
give him or her a rudimentary grasp
of scientific classification.

BACKBONE

Any living thing that is not a plant
is an animal.
Most animals that we know
have backbones.
A backbone is a row of bones along
the middle of the back.
Other bones are attached
to the backbone.
Together they make up a skeleton.

Here is a fish.

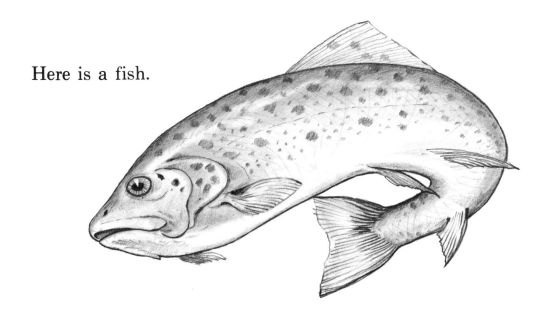

This is what is left on your plate after you
eat a fish.

Find the backbone.

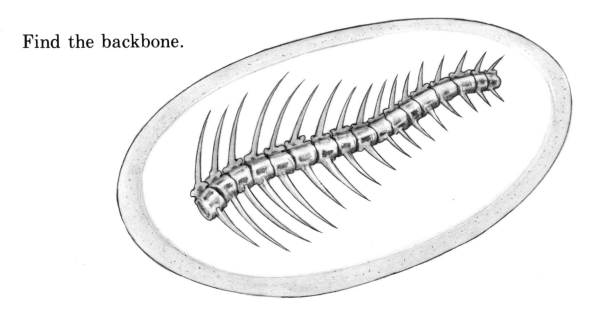

Here is a chicken.

This is what is left after you eat a chicken.
Find the backbone.

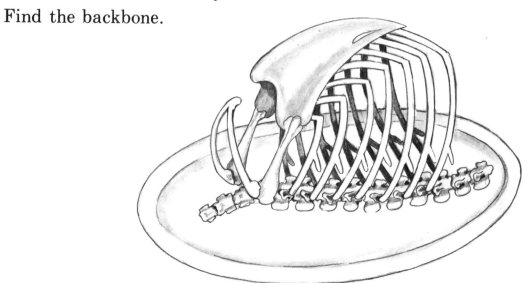

6

This is a snake's skeleton.
Find the backbone.

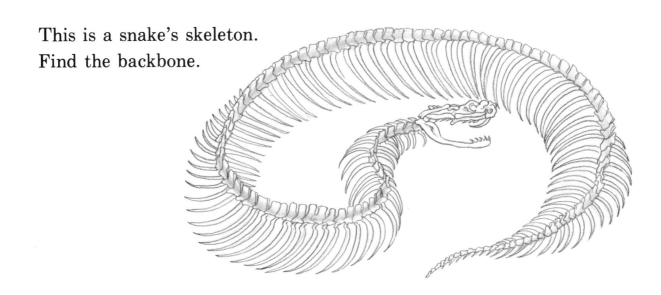

Look at the inside of this turtle's shell.

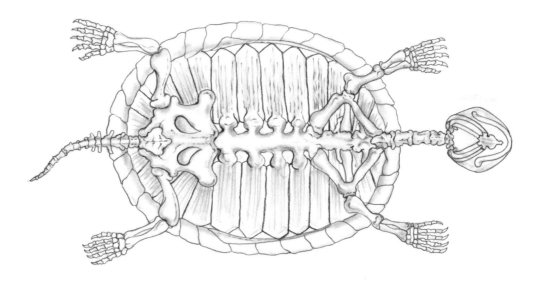

Can you see where the backbone has become
part of the shell?

Fish have backbones.

Amphibians (frogs, toads, and salamanders) have backbones.

Reptiles (snakes, lizards, turtles, and alligators) have backbones.

Birds have backbones.

Mammals (animals with hair or fur) have backbones.

All animals with backbones are called *vertebrates*.

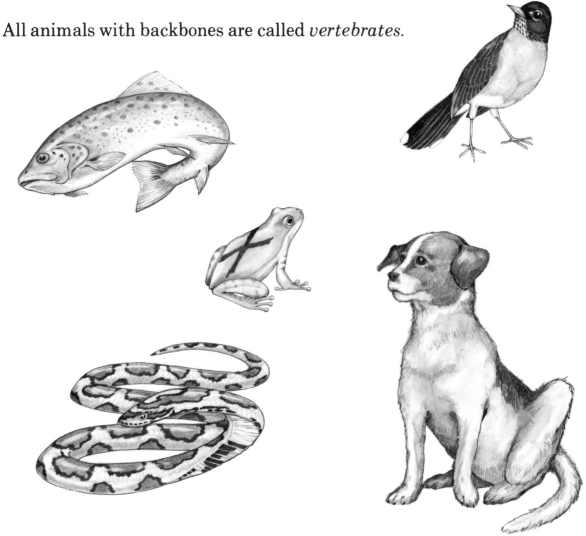

Although most of the animals we are familiar
with have backbones, 95% of all animals do not
have a backbone.

They are called *invertebrates* (in-VER-ta-brates).

Some invertebrates have a hard covering on the
outside of their bodies. This "outside
skeleton" gives the body shape and protects
the soft inside.

9

ARTHROPODS (AR-thro-pods)

Here are five animals with an outside skeleton.
They are in a group called *arthropods*.

They are different from all other invertebrates
because they have jointed legs.

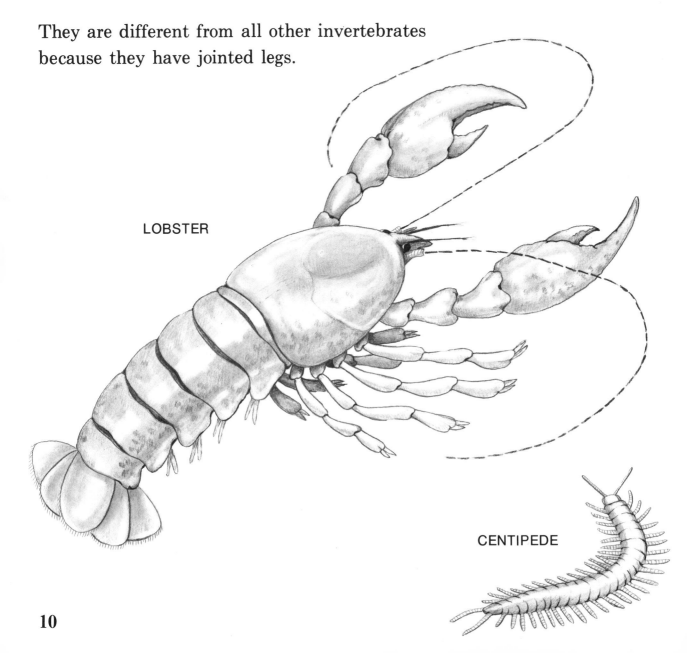

LOBSTER

CENTIPEDE

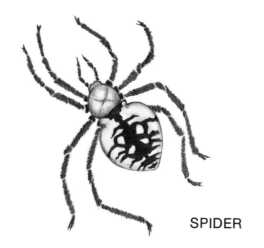

SPIDER

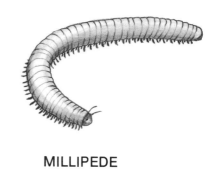

MILLIPEDE

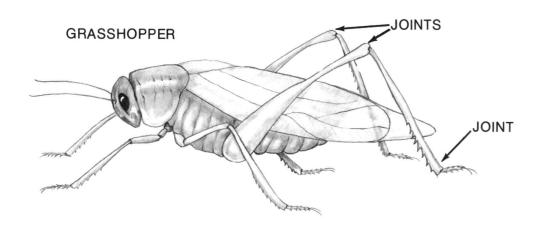

GRASSHOPPER

JOINTS

JOINT

The joints make it possible for the animal
to walk, swim, or jump.
Look for the joints in the legs.

11

All arthropods with six legs are called *insects*.

BUTTERFLY

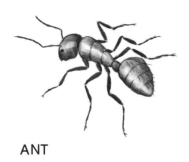

ANT

FLY

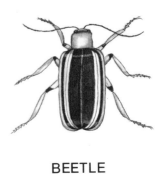

BEETLE

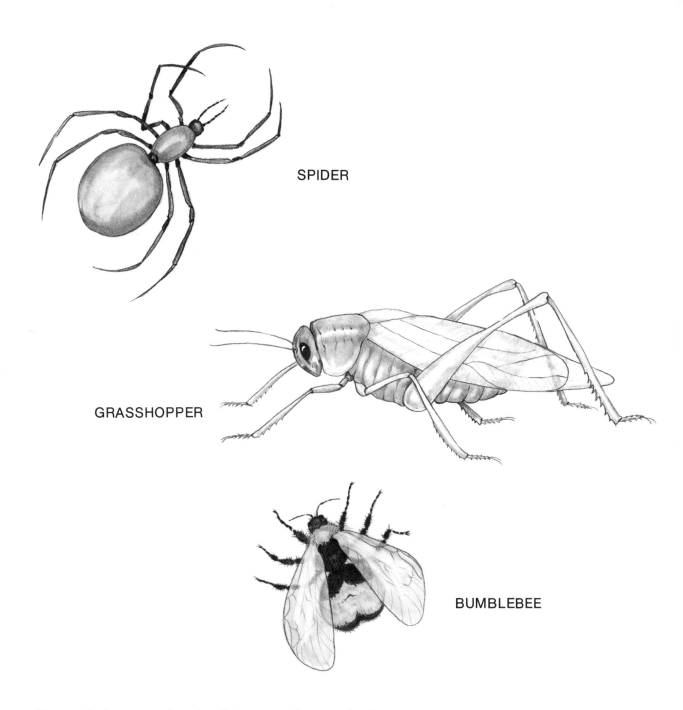

SPIDER

GRASSHOPPER

BUMBLEBEE

One of these animals does not have six legs.
Did you find it?
How many legs does the spider have?

The spider is not an insect because it has eight legs.

Are these insects?
Count the legs.

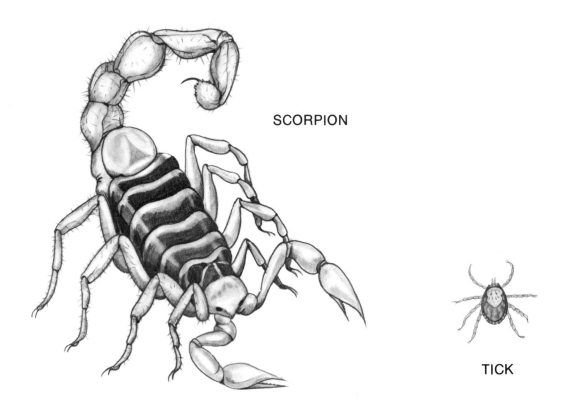

SCORPION

TICK

All arthropods with eight legs are called *arachnids* (a-RAK-nids).

Here are two animals with many legs.
Centipedes (SEN-ti-peeds) have fewer legs
than millipedes (MIL-li-peeds).
Which is which?

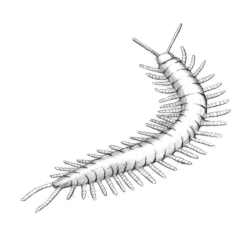

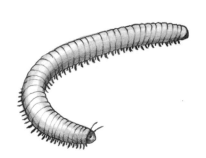

Arthropods with many jointed legs are either
centipedes or millipedes.

These invertebrates are also arthropods.
But you cannot tell them by counting their legs.
Count their antennae (an-TEN-ee) or feelers.
All arthropods with two pair of antennae are
called *crustaceans* (krus-TAY-shuns).

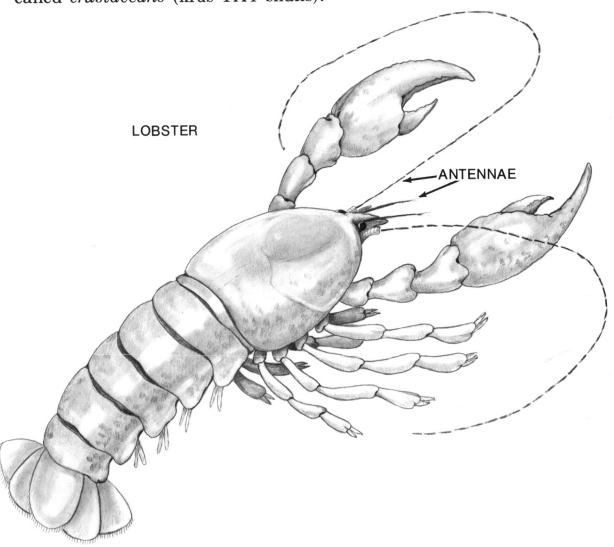

LOBSTER

ANTENNAE

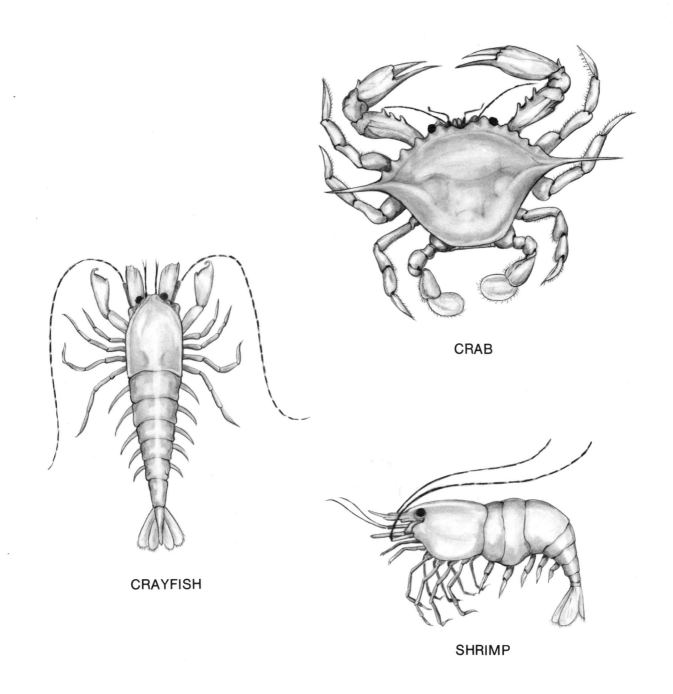

CRAB

CRAYFISH

SHRIMP

ECHINODERMS (e-KINE-o-derms)

Here are other invertebrates with a hard
covering. This time it is a spiny skin.
They are not arthropods because they do not
have jointed legs. Invertebrates with a spiny
skin are called *echinoderms*.

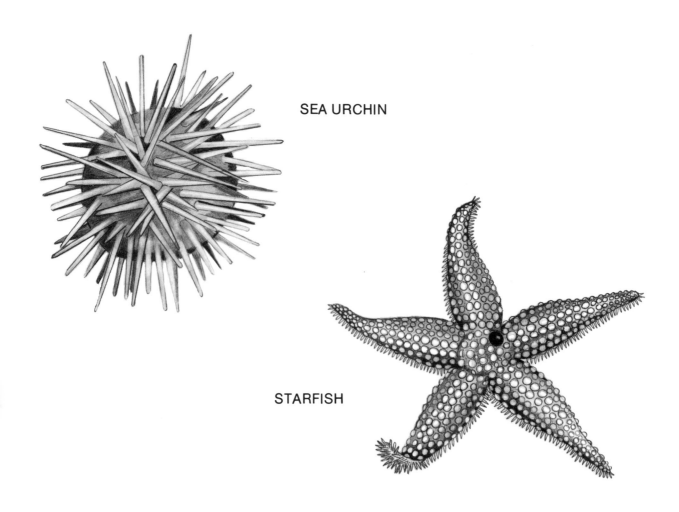

SEA URCHIN

STARFISH

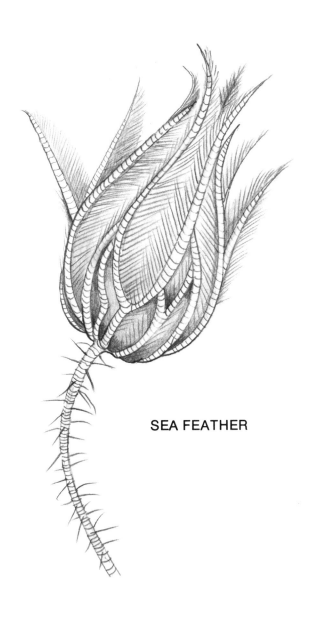

SEA FEATHER

SAND DOLLAR

Find the animal that looks like a star.
Find the animal that looks like a pincushion.
Find the animal with a flower design on the top.
Find the animal that looks as though it was
made of feathers.

MOLLUSKS (MOL-lusks)

These invertebrates do not have jointed legs.
They do not have a spiny skin.
But they do have a hard outside covering.
It is a shell made of lime
which covers the soft insides of the animal.

Some have two shells.

CLAM

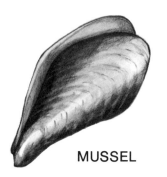

MUSSEL

SCALLOP

Some have one shell.

SNAIL

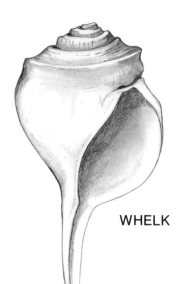

WHELK

PERIWINKLE

Here are two exceptions to the rule. These animals
have no outside shell but their soft
insides are very much like clams, oysters,
and snails. So they are put in the same group.

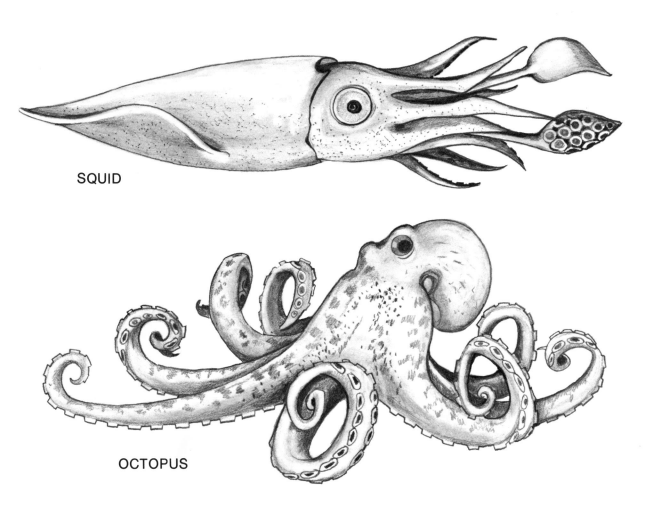

SQUID

OCTOPUS

All these invertebrates are called *mollusks*.

WORMS

Each of these worms belongs in a different group of invertebrates. Can you see any difference between them?

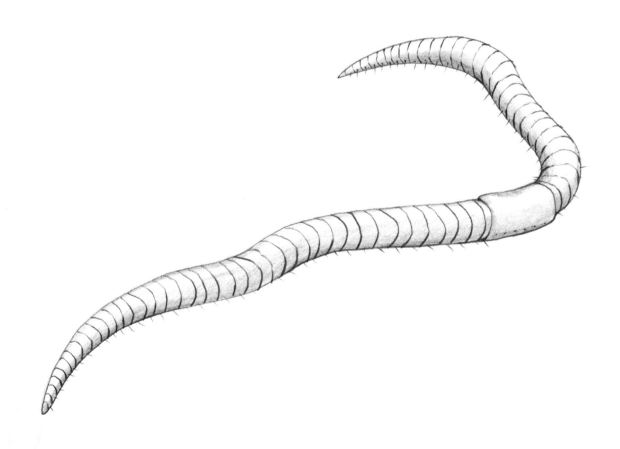

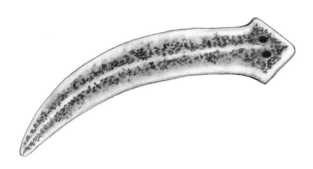

Which worm has rings around its body?
Which worm has a flat body?
Which worm is long and round like an eel?

The ringed worms are called *annelids* (AN-nel-ids).
The flat worms are called *platyhelminthes* (pla-tee-hel-MIN-theez).
The round worms are called *nemathelminthes* (ne-ma-thel-MIN-theez).

COELENTERATES (se-LEN-ter-rets)

This group of invertebrates has tentacles
that can sting. Look for the tentacles on the
sea anemone, jelly fish, hydra, and coral.

These invertebrates are called *coelenterates*.

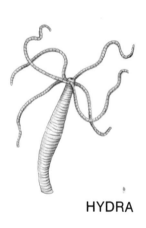

HYDRA

JELLYFISH

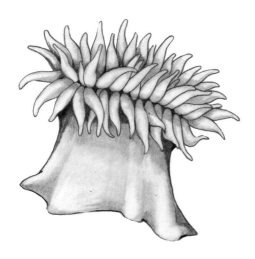

SEA ANEMONE

CORAL

Do you know two animals with tentacles
that do not sting?

Hint: See page 21.

SPONGES (SPUN-jes)

Sponges are another group of invertebrates.
The body of a sponge is a simple sac with many
holes. Water and food enter through these
holes and go out through a single large
opening.

The body wall is stiffened with a kind of
skeleton made of either glassy or chalky
needles, or spongy fibers.

The Venus Flower Basket is a glassy sponge.

The Vase-shaped sponge is a chalky sponge.

The Elephant's Ear sponge is a spongy sponge.

You can wash with an Elephant's Ear sponge
but the other two will scratch.

PROTOZOA (pro-ta-ZO-a)

These invertebrates called *protozoa* live in water and soil.
They are so small that most can only be seen
under a microscope.
They are one-celled animals. (A cell is the
smallest unit of life. Other animals are made
of many cells.)

There are three main kinds of protozoa
and they can be told apart by the way they move.

One kind moves little hairs (*cilia*)
like tiny oars.

One kind moves by beating a whiplike thread.

One kind moves by changing its shape.

Which is which?

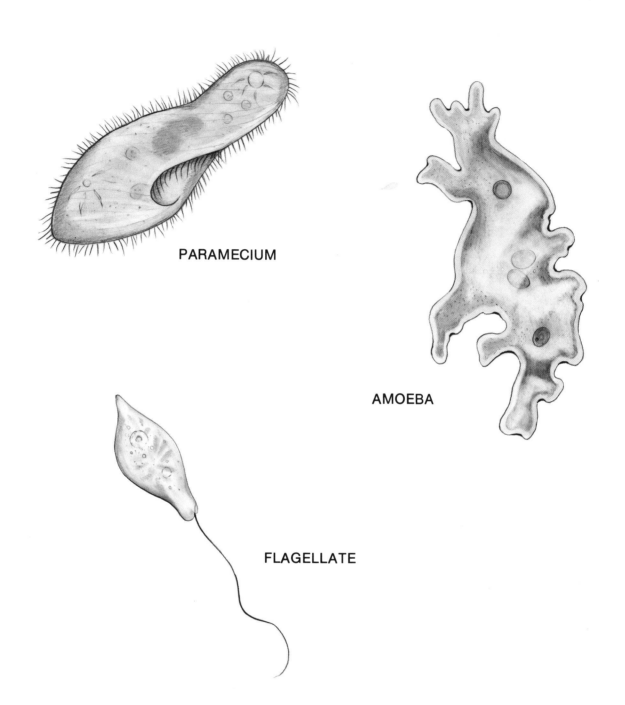

PARAMECIUM

AMOEBA

FLAGELLATE

29

INVERTEBRATES

Arthropods have jointed legs.

Echinoderms have spiny skins.

Mollusks have shells that cover soft bodies.

Annelids are ringed worms.

Nemathelminthes are round worms.

Platyhelminthes are flat worms.

Coelenterates have tentacles that sting.

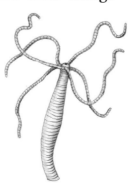 

Sponges are simple sacs with pores.

Protozoa are single-celled animals.

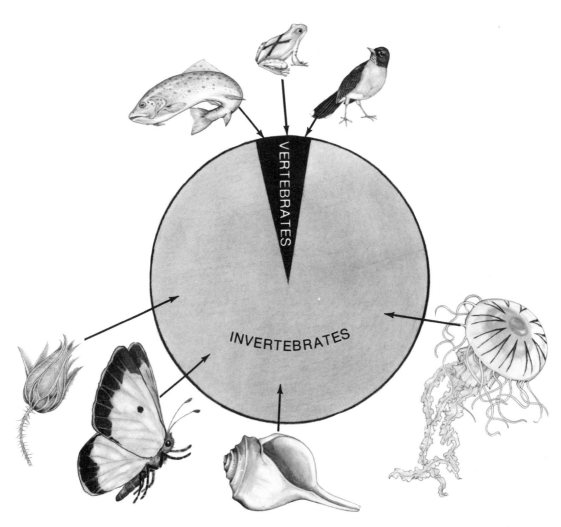

There are over one million different kinds of animals in the world.

Only 50,000 are vertebrates.

The rest are invertebrates.